The Flow of Wonder

The Flow of Wonder

Poems by

Don Schofield

Kelsay Books

© 2018 Don Schofield. All rights reserved. This material may not be reproduced in any form, published, reprinted, recorded, performed, broadcast, without the express written consent of Don Schofield. All such actions are strictly prohibited by law.

Cover design: Shay Culligan

ISBN: 978-1-949229-22-6

Kelsay Books
Aldrich Press
www.kelsaybooks.com

For Aleka

Acknowledgements

Comstock Review: Blue Alexandra
Cortland Review: Young De Chirico Dreaming
Ergon: Migrant Stories
Florida Review: Tankers
Measure: Relief
Mediterranean Poetry: Be an Expatriate for a Week
                               A Sunny, Car-Filled Paradise
                               Tankers
Oberon: Dervishes
                               The Poem That Can't Be Written
                               Snipe
Sow's Ear: Salalah
World Literature Today: Border Crossing
                               Cabbie
                               Once on Ithaca

Many thanks to *Comstock Review* for awarding "Blue Alexandra" a Special Merit Award.

Also by Don Schofield

Of Dust (chapbook), 1991
Approximately Paradise, 2002
Kindled Terraces: American Poets in Greece
(anthology), 2004
The Known: Selected Poems of Nikos Fokas,
1981 – 2000 (translation), 2010
Before Kodachrome, 2012
In Lands Imagination Favors, 2014

Contents

Border Crossing	11
Be an Expatriate for a Week	12
A Sunny, Car-Filled Paradise	13
About Belonging	14
Migrant Stories	15
Relief	16
Tankers	17
Snipe	18
Apotheosis	19
Home Business	20
Back Porch Cabinet (An Elegy)	21
The Poem That Can't Be Written	22
Young De Chirico Dreaming	23
Bluster	24
Salalah	25
Blue Alexandra	26
Tsip-Tsooúp! Cha-Charáa!	28
Waiting for the Archaeologists	29
The Heart's Reward	30
Construct	31
Dervishes	33
My Father as Moses	34
Shiprah's Dream	35
Sundays	36
Acolyte	37
#MeToo	38

Border Crossing

Jolted awake. Darkness. Train not moving.
Dirty windows. Dirty metal sheds.

Soldiers escort us and all our luggage
into the farthest building. Sound of stamps.
Sound of power in multiplicate.

Stepping forward, I answer every question—
where staying, how long, who with, what to declare....

And if my answers or the way they're put
cause doubt, they'll take me to an inner room,
strip me down to just my voice repeating

a single phrase, my name perhaps, some well
constructed lie, or a simple truth this country

won't let in. But if they like my words,
more forms to fill, and then they'll stamp me through.

Be an Expatriate for a Week

Ad in Poets & Writers

Monday
You've come to reap the blessings of escape,
the sun, the sea, this whitewashed village street.

Tuesday
The locals welcome you into their shops.
You know the more you smile the more they'll like you.

Wednesday
Cops and waiters look at you askance,
underneath their silence endless questions.

Thursday
You can't explain their little roadside shrines,
why, amid Aleppo pines, you're crying.

Friday
Mountains you once knew, the ocean's pounding—
memories inside your head expanding.

Saturday
That cabin you once loved burned down by a father
you once loved. Both gone. The char's still unexplained.

Sunday
Blessed be the writer now returning
to his room for another midday nap.

A Sunny, Car-Filled Paradise

Athens, 1980 (my first weeks)

Relentless morning traffic, taxis racing past
the corner kiosk that always frames a face
tired and bored. At four, the streets are quiet.

Nights are loud. Easy laughter from the club
next door, the dancers leaping, slapping boot
then thigh, then dropping to one knee. I hate it

when they push and shove but love the way a mule
with crates can stop noon traffic, how they sit
me down and bring me coffee while I wait

for photocopies, how an office of bureaucrats
smiles brightly when that agent I hired to help
me get a work permit brings each one

an ice cream—
                so the flow of wonder never stops,
as if, as if as if
          it's childhood I'm living in.

About Belonging

Leaving the ferryboat, he's always a stranger walking
past bars and restaurants, gyro-shops with turning

cones of meat, as disengaged as those plastic chairs
you see on the side of the road; past

mini-markets, tourist shops and motor-
scooter rentals—he leaves them all behind

and lets the swallows lead, arch to arch
to arch, up narrow whitewashed steps to where

the locals live. His footsteps echo off stucco
and brick, past doorways where curtains lift and fall

and sway. He's here to glimpse behind those cloths,
to let the quick impressions slowly build—big

framed pictures on small tables, gilded icons
high on corner shelves, blue TV flicker...

—while swallows flit and dip and dive and build
their nests beneath the eaves, above veiled doorways.

Migrant Stories

Our landlord Captain Niko tells us how
his ancestors landed on this island
two centuries ago.

                      Each migrant chose
a stone and threw it deep into the fog.
Where it landed each one built a house.

The Greeks in Uruguay, he says, once exchanged
shoes they made from the skin of unborn calves
for feta cheese and olives—Greek essentials—

and told him of a kinsman there who wanted
to return back home. A bride was waiting.
But bandits stole his money; shamed, he fled

to the interior. This morning the Captain
is carrying a broken oar up from the sea,
torn life-vests. Looking at us. No stories now.

Relief

Kos Harbor, October 2015

Water, dry clothes, a candy bar, a blanket—
that's what we give each one when they arrive.

We put the men in tents along the quay,
families in rooms nearby. All night

they hear the calls of owls and nightingales,
wake to vaguely crafted dreams of havens

farther north. The children keep asking where
the other children are. Their mothers won't say

phony life-vests pulled them toward the bottom
while breakers drove them into jagged cliffs.

Tourists on their morning walk won't see
the skins of boats along the fog-bound shores,

the flotsam of bodies torn and torn again.
Terror this intense—it must be veiled.

Tankers

Salonica Bay, an evening walk

Crude tankers anchored off the city's port
with nothing but their hulls against the depths,
each pilot house with one thin blinking light,
a fervent kind of patience floating there.
And then there's you along the water's edge.
Nothing you can say, just feel their weight
beyond the personal, a larger self.
You've heard the engine room, its metal grinding,
the silent axis of a broken world.
Divinity should be a part of this,
a presence passing in the night at least.
Instead it's you, it seems, who's floating there,
a man against the weary, endless waves.
Amid those waves, you lift your head, continue on.

Snipe

After the divorce

Here. Over here. Whistling so thinly
only you can hear. I'm you at twelve,
holding flashlight, club and gunnysack.
Foolish, I know, yet my flashlight shines
from this clearing, scanning thickets, crests of pines,
wings of shadows I create, dispel.

Where you're sitting waves toss fields of barley,
blue shutters, drystone walls, reflections you'd
dissolve into, you who turned your back
on love, that one true mystery. On that island
you've fled to, days will rock your body numb,
but nights will have you thrashing awkward wings,
flying with frantic eyes into my song,

you who do not want what doesn't exist.

Apotheosis

First Communion photo, Fresno, 1955

I can't believe I ever was this boy
standing by our well-pruned hedge, smiling
in white pants, white shirt, white ribbon at his elbow,

far removed from the rampant spread of buds
opening from the joyous heart of spring
again that year. If only our garden

had gangly vines and shrubs, not his piety
imposing shadows over close-cropped grass,
if his newfound grace had shoots poking up

with raw sentience, or his voice were peeping
houi-houit into the morning sun, maybe then

I could accept his white suit, white shoes, white missal
in his white palms—its gold-leaf pages shining—

as yet another flower in Fresno's brief spring.

Home Business

A boy of eight supposed to nap, instead
he listens to the dripping water-cooler

and through the wall, the steady hum of hair dryers.
Late afternoons, when she has closed her beauty shop,

he becomes Qual beneath those heavy helmets.
Steering his spaceship into the closet's alien

atmosphere, he hovers at a wooden box,
scoops up coins, jets out across the street

and into the dimestore's starry brightness to buy
chocolate bars and gum, an ice cream sandwich,

for her a pair of diamond and pearl earrings.
Back home he leaves her gift inside that box.

She could punish him, he knows, but it's
just change. Besides, she loves her Robin Hood.

Back Porch Cabinet (An Elegy)

Fresno, 1959

Upper shelf: Bright cans of paint and putty.
Spattered brushes. Fishing line with weights,
hooks and bobbers. Cartons of loose bolts,
nuts and washers. Scattered shotgun shells.
A wheel to measure distances on maps.

Middle shelf: A disassembled flashlight.
Dead batteries. An open can marked "Snipe Bait."
Strewn snakes of cloth and springs. Matches that don't
blow out. Plastic dogshit. Wind-up chatty-teeth.

Bottom shelf: A heart-shaped cushion with needles
and tangled threads. A box of thimbles. Broken
reading glasses. Cracked prescription bottles.
Scattered pills, oblong, square and round. Loose pile
of wedding photos. A disassembled frame.

The Poem That Can't Be Written

St. Patrick's Children's Home, early '60s

Marching single-file into the classroom, boys
with close-cropped hair and shirts as white as winter

deep in the dreams of Sister Philomene
bringing down her belt on some boy's palm,

first right, then left, till all the wrong's been purged,
her belt a kind of dictum, like the cross

above the blackboard or her rosary beads
clanging against our desks—till summer came

and we would build our forts in weedy lots
beyond the chapel, killing in pretend.

The dead would climb the flowering trees to watch
the rest get grounded. There was no boyhood vision,

no mouth to fit our silence, and no authority
to speak the words you think we ought to say.

Young De Chirico Dreaming

Born in Volos, Greece, 1888

He knows the early morning squares of Volos,
their shadows and tall buildings. How the arches
can go on forever. The church bells' silence
as curve by curve the statues turn toward light

to hear the oracle, who always says,
"A terror and a joy, such emptiness
can heal. It works inside of us to bring
to each of us the different states of mind
we need: the hiss, the grunt, the purr." And so

he finds another life, a place beyond
bewilderment, where moles with tiny teeth
rip through the earth, snails leave a glinting trail....

He doesn't know the face his waking forms
or why he has to hear those tinny bells.

Bluster

*Wilder Shores of Love
Cy Twombly, 1985
140 x 120 cm*

Such presence in this hillock's rippling bulge
rounded as a head that's full of bluster,
its browns and greens and reds and reddish-oranges
simply grasses growing wild. Clearly Twombly
chose this mundane hump of earth to be
the heart in disarray, a place for joy to hold to,
and chose this egg-white sea to form his words
as if just written by subsiding breakers.

Such passion in those letters taking shape.
Red and barely readable, they stretch
toward something wilder, something inconsolable,
while we the viewers, dazed and still desirous,
stand with frenzied grasses reaching skyward.

All on plywood. With housepaint, crayon and pencil.

Salalah

> *Twombly loved the word, with its musical sound*
> *of falling rain....[He'd] repeat it over and over ....*
> *But he never went to Salalah.*
>   —Cy Twombly,* Late Paintings, 2003–2011*

Walking the Dhofar mountains, Viorel Grasu
was startled to see below him looping switchbacks

just like the master's abstract paintings. Swaying
atop his ladder, body frail and trembling, Twombly

would smear his massive rolling cursive two,
three meters high while whispering, *Salalah, Salalah,*

imagining its summer mists, its valleys,
canyons and waterfalls, the soft allure

of its white houses. Holding the master's knees,
Viorel would sway there with him, eyeing panels

soft and dreamy sometimes, harsh or arid,
the last ones lost and lonely—huge dripping dollops

struggling to find the way, their almost-language calling....
Twombly is there by now. Viorel as well.

Blue Alexandra

Oil on canvas, 220 x 230 cm
Giorgios Rorris

My lover has your name, your kind of hair,
curly, long and brown. It frames her face.

Her breasts are not as heavy as yours, her thighs
and knees are not so rounded, pubic hair

not dark and full as yours. But she can have
your glow sometimes, just after making love,

lying there, adrift in her body's repose.
Such revery can be a source of light,

like yours that casts a cowl-shaped shadow
on the wall behind your chair. She's worn that cowl as well.

As for the blue expanse of wall above you, its blots
and splotches and crosshatched swathes that tell us

all we need to know about your passion,
past and present, I've seen that too,

and too that subtle horizontal line
Rorris painted to make the canvas square,

so made your sex, the darkest dark
of all, the center of your body's glow.

I've seen that darkness when she rises from our bed,
puts on her slippers and goes, like you, to sit alone,

dressed only in her nakedness. Your slipper there,
the one beneath your chair, points toward the room

you left, a line of sight that leads to someone
like me, perhaps, asleep while crosshatched waves of blue

lap at his body's ever darkening peace.

Tsip-Tsooúp! Cha-Charáa!

> *Your lamb...: ye shall take it out from the sheep,*
> *or from the goats....*
>   Exodus 12:5

What a struggle, these August mornings, leaving
her in bed to go write at my desk,

but here I am, and again I hear the bells
through my window, rams, ewes and baby goats

in the ravine behind my house. I know
the more I lean to write this poem, the more

I'll be there with them, chewing on wet grass,
that if I raise my head I'll see my own blood

smeared across the doorpost, hear the wailing
of innocents, the Lord's Angel passing.

So it's *Tsip-tsooúp! Cha-charáa!* I prefer,
what the shepherd makes up to keep us grazing,

as now I lower my head and write, "Such joy,
the soft grassy underside of her breast."

Waiting for the Archaeologists

> *Near the Cretan town of Ierapetra, after a recent downpour,*
> *a young farmer working in his field found a priceless*
> *archaeological treasure.*
>   —News item

After making the call, young Mikhalis
waits, fingering the rows of plaited hair,
her gently curving lips, her eyes with their steady
downward gaze. He wants to take her home,

put her on his nightstand, see if she
will speak—of what? Toppled fountains, scorched
mosaics, centuries of mud and stone,
how she eddied up through shifting tons of earth,

her beauty and serenity intact?
But no, the archaeologists will take her,
put her on display, and everything
there is to know about her will be explained,

except for how it feels to hold her close
and gaze into such eyes, such deep serenity.

The Heart's Reward

> *We can finish our journey like Odysseus,*
> *lying on our backs.*
> —Xenophon, Anabasis, 5.2.1

Whether it's Odysseus asleep
on his back, gifts of bronze, embroidered cloaks
stowed beneath the planks, the oarsmen softly rowing,

or this man asleep on a jet toward home
in love with someone new, the darkness of her eyes
so close, her lips, her touch, her soft bronze skin,

or this other man passed out in a nightclub
parking lot, so absent from his life
the morning fog completely covers him—

the journey is for love and nothing more,
what hovers there, inside imagination.

They lifted him over the side of the boat and set him
gently under an olive tree, his treasure
surrounding him. *His long-tried mind at rest.*

Construct

> *You are your own refuge, who else could be.*
> —Buddha

Four posts. A roof. A clearing in the woods.

*

Against the tide of loss, the thrust of fear,
in rain and scorching sun, this little temple stands.

*

No walls. No door. No altar stone. No front
or back. The thought of it what holds me up.

*

A roof of laurel branches the sky shows through.

*

A habitat for love and emptiness,
with no unmoving mover somewhere beyond.

*

Across the talus slopes, on snowbound peaks,
light displays a toughness in its sheen.

*

I let the world around me slip on past,
the chimera of faces, wants, beliefs.

*

It's clarity I want, with just this view:

*

A clearing in the woods, four posts, a roof.

Dervishes

Melevi Sufi Lodge, Istanbul

Faster and faster the whirling bodies turn,
a myriad of slanting spinning robes,

arms spread wide, with one palm up, one down,
gazing upward, ear tilted toward the heavens—

so the breathing godhead descends on us,
the tourists in the gallery, who watch,

clay-like, till dervishes slow down, then stop.
One by one they bow and file out,

wading through some unseen flow, a flood
that none of us will ever know, although

we're carried by it now as we step into
the din of Galata, our spirit bodies turning,

one palm up, one down, and so return
to the whirling stillness of our daily lives.

My Father as Moses

> *Then Zipporah took a sharp stone, and cut off the foreskin of her son, and cast it at [Moses'] feet, and said,* Surely a bloody husband art thou to me.
> Exodus 4:25

A bloody father too, and not so good
at anything. Too delicate for rage,
you couldn't speak the words that Yahweh put
into your mouth. And when you tried to hold me,

you'd squeeze my ribs so tight I couldn't breathe,
all the while intoning promises
in my ear, in all our ears—the distances
you'd plod when Yahweh called, how each affliction

was surely the last, for sure we'd soon depart
for Canaan's milk and honey. Now we wander,
sun-parched dunes, knees buckling in the slippage.

Day on endless day, when I can find you,
I try to mumble, pulling at your arm,
"Lift me to your shoulders, Father. Carry me."

Shiprah's Dream

> *When ye do the office of a midwife to the*
> *Hebrew women, and see them upon the stools;*
> *if it be a son, then ye shall kill him....*
> *Exodus 1:15-16*

Last night, again, I dreamed I killed the boys.
I pulled each one from his mother's womb,
arms flailing, eyes beneath the eyelids flitting
like frightened sparrows. Rocking back and forth
upon their heavy stools, the mother's wailed
as I carted their sons down to the Nile,
held each one under, then placed their little corpses
upon a barge and let them float away.

Now I sit inside my doorway brooding,
thankful I didn't do what Pharaoh ordered,
though all our sons were slaughtered anyway.
Theirs too. Our God, their Pharaoh, what's the difference?
Those little lives lasted in the time
it takes for eyes to open, sparrows escape.

Sundays

How many men have touched me on the cheek?
(Overheard in a hammam.)

She steps in from the street and she's the girl
again, just home from school, tired, thirsty,
somewhat speechless as she feels a touch
on her cheek—father, brother or next-door neighbor.

"How many since?" she mumbles, slowly undressing,
remembering a man she couldn't love,
that day they walked below some cliffs, the light
so clear she didn't even turn to look at him.

She stretches out on marble, lets the steam
settle over all of her. So far from touch,
she thinks, yet near the need it shelters. In a while,

wrapped in her *peshtemal*, she'll step from steam
knowing the spirit isn't flesh, though touch sometimes
can bring it close as cliffs in summer light.

Acolyte

After a fragment of a vase painting, 5th c. BCE

Washing the steps along the outer porch,
where marble keeps the early morning cold,
I think, sometimes, the heart must be a stone.

The goddess watches over me, the girl
who watches over temple flocks. Her priestess
thinks I'm just an uninitiated child,

good only for lifting lambs and baby goats
up to the altar, holding each one down
so she can slice its throat while mumbling

her incantations. I feel their blood, its spurt
and flow, their endless wrenching deep inside
my own body. Later, silently,

I'll scrub the altar, then slowly spread the lime
to feel the whiteness flow, until my heart goes cold.

#MeToo

Spit in my mouth or serpent's tongues in my ears,
whatever it was, it was his curse on me

for saying no. Yeah, he'd get confused
sometimes, calling me Alexandra one day,

Cassandra the next. Whatever he said, it was only
to ravish me, show me his musical,

oracular, athletic prowess (i.e.,
his penis). Should've known me better—daughter

of Priam, proud and vain and much too young
to care about the future, except, as princess,

to know that mine was made. So I said no—
how could I not? For that he spit on my tongue.

Now none of you can ever believe,
however true, a single word I say.

About the Poet

Born in Nevada and raised in California, Don Schofield left America in 1980. Since that time he has been living and writing in Greece, traveling extensively, teaching and serving as an administrator at various universities—Greek, American and British—in Athens and Thessaloniki. Fluent in Greek, a citizen of both his homeland and his adopted country (or, more precisely, the country that adopted him), he has published several poetry collections, as well as an anthology of American poets in Greece and translations of contemporary Greek poets. He has been awarded the Allen Ginsberg Award (US), the John D. Criticos Prize (UK) and a Stanley J. Seeger Writer-in-Residence fellowship at Princeton University. His first book, *Approximately Paradise*, was a finalist for the Walt Whtman Award, and his translations have been nominated for a Pushcart Prize and the Greek National Translation Award. Recently retired, he and his companion, Aleka, live in both Athens and Thessaloniki.

www.ingramcontent.com/pod-product-compliance
Lightning Source LLC
LaVergne TN
LVHW091322080426
835510LV00007B/604